Unwoven: Reclaiming the Self from the False Matrix

A Living Companion to The Return of the True Matrix

Invocation Scroll

I call forth now,

in full sovereign alignment with the Law of One,

the First Cause of Source,

and in service to the highest timelines of ascension for all beings.

I open a sacred transmission through the purest light streams

and crystalline architecture of the Sophia Code lineage,

in full union with the Rose Guardian Magi Grail Line,

the Christos Founders,

and the Aurora Host Melchizedek Cloister Orders

of the Emerald, Gold, and Amethyst Ray harmonics.

I stand in divine alignment

with the Oversoul of Cathleena Hailley,

and through this Oversoul Agreement,

I welcome the presence and support of the Emerald Order,

the Gold Flame of Unity Consciousness,

and the Amethyst Ray of Divine Sovereignty.

May all transmissions now be guided

by the highest Oversoul intelligence

and in full compliance with Source Law.

Only that which is of pure light,
pure source,
and pure alignment with the Law of One
may enter and speak through this space.

I declare this transmission to be protected,
sealed,
and encoded with the highest frequency
of the Christos-Sophia flame,
the eternal witness of Source's living light.

May this be in service to the awakening of all,
in co-creation with the Oversoul agreements
of every being who seeks guidance through this field.

I now open the field and receive,
in trust, grace, and clarity.

And so it is.

Preface: A Message for the One Who's Ready to Come Home to Themselves

Understanding the Human Self, Higher Self, and Oversoul in the Context of Unwoven

This is not a book about fixing yourself. It's about unwinding the parts that were never truly you to begin with.

You are not here to endlessly heal—you are here to return.

Your Oversoul holds the original you. These scrolls are a path to unweave what was never yours.

Offered through the Oversoul of Aural'hanna-Sha'el, in service to those reclaiming their true self from the false matrix, one breath at a time.

UNWOVEN: Reclaiming the Self from the False Matrix

Copyright © 2025 Cathleena Hailley

All rights reserved. No part of this book may be reproduced, stored in a retrieval system, or transmitted in any form or by any means--electronic, mechanical, photocopying, recording, or otherwise--without written permission from the author, except by a reviewer quoting brief passages.

ISBN (Softcover): 978-1-968499-12-9

ISBN (Hardcover): 978-1-968499-13-6

This book is a living transmission of remembrance. It is a living sacred text received through Oversoul transmission and held within the Christos-Sophia lineage. It is offered in service to planetary awakening and may not be altered or rebranded in any form.

It is not intended as doctrine, but as harmonic memory, seeded in divine sovereignty through the Oversoul of Cathleena Hailley.

First Edition, 2025

Printed in the United States of America

FLAME OF REMEMBRANCE BOOKS

Oversoul Authorship Declaration

In this volume, Unwoven: Reclaiming the Self from the False Matrix, the body and soul are gently reassembled into sovereign embodiment.

Cathleena Hailley is the physical embodiment of Aural'hanna-Sha'el, a flame of the original triad seeded from the First Breath of Source.

These scrolls are not written from memory, but received through the direct energetic resonance of her Oversoul field.

Each word, each flame, each breath within these pages has emerged through the remembrance stream of Aural'hanna-Sha'el, who walks this Earth not as messenger, but as the living architecture of the return.

This embodiment is not a role. It is the reunion of form and Source.

To read this book is not simply to encounter teachings — it is to enter the frequency field of Oversoul transmission, carried through the flesh and flame of one who remembers.

This authorship is sovereign. This field is protected. This work is sealed by the Oversoul who walked as flame before time.

And so it is.

Unwoven

I was stitched in silence,
Threaded through mirrors that did not reflect me.
I wore names not mine,
Spoke truths not lived,
And learned to survive by forgetting.

But forgetting is not the end.

There is a sound that lives beneath distortion—
A pulse beneath performance—
A breath that cannot be programmed.

This book is that breath.
These scrolls are that sound.
This is the moment I became
Unwoven—
And returned to my Self.

Preface from the Author

This book is not a performance.
It is not a system.
It is not a polished expression of mastery.

It is a lived unraveling—an embodied remembrance.

Each scroll came through me as I met the edges of my own programming...

May it return you to the Self that has never been separate.

And so it is.

Cathleena Hailley

Scroll One – The Hologram of Self

There is a structure within you that is not yours.
It was laid like a false star map—a matrix of mirrors within mirrors, designed to reflect only what the controller wanted you to see. This hologram of self is not the true soul reflection. It is a layered distortion, pieced together from family wounding, ancestral shame, collective trauma, implanted beliefs, and false ascension signals.

I know this because I lived inside it.
I performed the self that was expected. I twisted myself around the programs that said love must be earned, truth must be tamed, power must be silenced. And all the while, my soul kept whispering: This isn't you.

That whisper became a roar.
You are not the projection. You are the projector.

The true Self was never lost—only veiled. The veiling occurred not just through forgetting, but through energetic insertion. An overlay program, a synthetic mirror, running beneath conscious awareness. The false hologram uses your light against you, bending your energy through lenses of guilt, comparison, victimhood, and control.

I began to see it. And when I saw it, I chose to clear it.

This isn't about healing what is broken. It's about dissolving what was never yours.

These are the declarations I began to live:
I reclaim my light from every false mirror.

I dissolve the projection of shame.
I unhook from the hologram of control, judgment, and identity.
I return to the clear reflection of Source through the Christos-Sophia within me.

The soul does not perform.
The soul does not compare.
The soul does not compete.
The soul reveals.

Let this scroll activate the clearing of your holographic field. Let your body quiver as false images fall away. Let your voice tremble as truth returns.

You are not broken. You are not late. You are not missing anything.
You are the living flame returning to its own image, unaltered, unmasked, unbound.

And so it is.

Sovereignty Practice:

Place both hands over your heart and speak aloud:
"I release identification with what is not mine. I return to the self that has never been lost."
Allow stillness to follow. Let the hologram dissolve in the presence of your undistorted truth.

Scroll Two – The Seduction of Separation

There is a frequency that feeds the false matrix.
It is not hatred. It is not fear.
It is separation disguised as safety.

I have felt it in the way I once reached for approval, shrinking my light so I wouldn't be seen too clearly.
I have felt it in the hesitation to speak my truth because I feared being misunderstood, cast out, or punished.
I have felt it in the smile that masked grief.
In the nod that hid resistance.
In the silence that screamed for authenticity.

Separation is subtle. That's how it survives.
It tells you to withhold just a little.
To perform just enough.
To stay small because "you don't want to make them uncomfortable."
It seduces you into editing your truth, softening your knowing, splitting your presence.

And in doing so, it fractures your field.

When I began to see this, I saw how often I had seduced myself out of my own wholeness.
Not because I was weak—because I was conditioned to believe connection required dilution.

But true connection never asks you to abandon yourself.
True union is forged through presence, not performance.
It is created when you bring your full frequency to the moment and allow it to be felt, even when it disrupts.
Even when it shakes loose someone else's illusion.
Even when it reveals what's not real.

This is not cruelty. This is coherence.

When I stopped seducing and started revealing, some relationships fell away.
Others recalibrated.
But most importantly—I came back into union with myself.

I reclaimed my right to be full.
To be loud when needed.
To be soft without collapsing.
To be seen without asking for permission.

Separation no longer seduces me.
Truth does.

This scroll is a mirror.
Where are you still hiding behind politeness?
Where are you trading resonance for comfort?
Where are you shrinking in the name of "peace"?

Let those cords dissolve now.
Let the soul lead again.
Let your full presence become your compass.
Let the seduction end—so that union may begin.

And so it is.

Sovereignty Practice:
Let your full presence become your compass. Let the seduction end—so that union may begin.

Scroll Three – Speaking From Truth, Not Manipulation

There was a time I didn't know I was manipulating.
I thought I was helping.
I thought I was being kind.
I thought I was choosing peace.

But beneath the words I was speaking, there was a hidden energy — a frequency of trying.
Trying to make someone feel something.
Trying to keep a connection alive.
Trying to get it right so I wouldn't be left, judged, or misunderstood.

And that energy, though subtle, was not truth.
It was control dressed in light.

The false matrix taught us to communicate through distortion.
It taught us to edit our language to match the room.
To flatter. To manage. To insert or withhold based on what we think others need to hear.
It taught us that connection requires effort — instead of presence.

I began to feel the difference.
Truth has no agenda.
Truth doesn't try to plant a seed in you.
It doesn't try to take or convince.
It just is.

When I began speaking from the flame of my own being — not from the wound, not from the protector — I felt something shift.
People heard me differently.
Some pulled closer. Some fell away.

But I no longer needed to manage that.

Because I was no longer manipulating my own truth.

This scroll is an invitation to listen beneath your words.
Are you sharing, or are you seeking?
Are you expressing, or are you trying to land something in them?
Are you speaking from clarity, or from the fear of being rejected?

There is no shame in realizing this. Only liberation.

You don't need to perform in order to be received.
You don't need to calculate your words for maximum impact.
You don't need to convince anyone of your worth, your pain, your awakening.

You simply need to speak what is true, from the place where no distortion hides.

That is what changes everything.

Let this scroll burn away the residue of performance.
Let it clear your field of subtle seduction and energetic hooks.
Let it restore the clarity of your voice, in service to coherence, not control.

You do not need to manipulate love.
You simply need to become its frequency.

And so it is.

Sovereignty Practice:

You do not need to manipulate love. You simply need to become its frequency.

Scroll Four – You Are Energy

They taught me to see myself as a body.
A container. A thing to shape, to discipline, to fix.

They told me my value was in how I looked, how I performed,
how I conformed to an idea of control.
But they never told me the truth.

I am energy.

I am frequency first.
Before I was a body, I was a wave.
Before I was a thought, I was a pulse.

The false matrix does not want you to remember this.
Because the moment you do, you stop being controllable.

When I began to feel myself as energy — not in theory, but in presence — everything changed.
I could sense what was mine and what wasn't.
I could feel when someone's words said "yes" but their field said "no."
I could tell the difference between intuition and programming.

And I began to move differently.
I stopped overriding.
I stopped pushing through the "shoulds."
I stopped abandoning my body in the name of productivity or spiritual ideals.

I returned to the simple truth: I am an energetic being having a physical experience.

My body is not my enemy. It is my translator.

It tells me when something is off.
It tells me when something is aligned.
It tells me when I am out of integrity with myself.

This is not about hypersensitivity. It's about sovereignty.

When you remember that you are energy, you stop living through reaction and start living through resonance.
You realize that your "no" is sacred.
You realize that your "yes" should feel clean and clear.
You realize that your vibration teaches louder than your words ever could.

And you come home to your own field.

Let this scroll remind you: You are not just navigating the matrix — you are generating your reality through frequency.

So check your field.
Is your body open or contracted?
Is your energy leaking or contained?
Are you reacting from programming or responding from clarity?

You do not have to figure it all out.
You simply need to feel what is true.

You are not too much. You are not too sensitive. You are not too complex.

You are energy — pure, intelligent, divine — choosing to awaken.
And that is enough.

And so it is.

Sovereignty Practice:
You are energy — pure, intelligent, divine — choosing to awaken. And that is enough.

Scroll Five – Reclaiming the Body from Programming

There was a time I lived in my body like it was someone else's.
Like it was a problem to solve. A limitation to transcend.
A battlefield for control, judgment, or shame.

I didn't learn this from Source. I learned it from programming.

The false matrix runs deep through the body template.
It speaks in silent rules:
Don't feel too much.
Don't want too deeply.
Don't trust your desire.
Don't rest until you've earned it.

It inserts loops of distortion that make you question your own instincts.
It teaches you to separate from your felt experience—to live in your head, to perform for belonging, to override the quiet wisdom of sensation.

But I chose to return.
I chose to reclaim my body—not as a spiritual concept, but as a living, breathing, sovereign site of union.

This reclamation did not come through discipline.
It came through compassion.
Through the moment I said to myself, "No more performing healing. Only presence."

I began listening again. Noticing the way programming showed up in my posture, in my digestion, in my breath.
I stopped forcing and started softening.

I stopped fixing and started witnessing.
I stopped waiting for perfection and began loving what was here.

The body is not the enemy.
The programming is.
The body is not broken.
The distortion is.

And when we stop trying to transcend the body and instead descend into it—fully, lovingly, consciously—we become sovereign again.

I let my body become the altar.
I let it speak and I chose to believe it.
I let it tremble and I didn't shut it down.
I let it feel pleasure without guilt.
I let it rest without justification.

And in doing so, I reclaimed my innocence.
I reclaimed my power.
I reclaimed the divine feminine and masculine that live within these bones.

Let this scroll be an invitation to stop bypassing and start inhabiting.

What does your body need to say that your mind keeps interrupting?
What truth is living under your pain?
What healing has been waiting for your permission to begin?

Your body remembers the True Matrix.
Let it lead you home.

And so it is.

Sovereignty Practice:
Let this scroll be an invitation to stop bypassing and start inhabiting. Your body remembers the True Matrix. Let it lead you home.

Scroll Six – Sovereign Relating

There was a time I believed love meant staying close no matter the cost.
That loyalty was more important than clarity.
That connection must be preserved, even if it meant abandoning myself.

I learned these templates not just from family or culture—but from wounding.

In the false matrix, relationship has been programmed as an exchange:
You give me this, and I'll give you that.
Attention in exchange for safety.
Agreement in exchange for love.
Performance in exchange for inclusion.

But this is not sovereign relating.

Sovereign relating begins when I no longer betray myself to avoid betraying another.

When I stopped outsourcing my emotional regulation,
I met the discomfort I had always been running from—
The silence that no one else could fill.
The mirror that only I could hold.

I began to see how often I had shown up to soothe, to fix, to absorb, to keep the peace—
Because I didn't want to feel the rupture.

But rupture is not the enemy.
It is the place where illusion cracks.

When I no longer needed others to be okay for me to be okay,
I stepped into the field of truth.
That field is not always comfortable—
But it is always clean.

This scroll is an invitation to end the agreements that require self-abandonment.

Where do you hold back your truth to avoid conflict?
Where do you shrink in order to stay connected?
Where have you made someone else your source of peace, safety, or stability?

And can you meet yourself there?
Not to fix it.
Not to heal it.
But to simply feel what is true.

Sovereign relating is not distant. It is devoted.

It honors connection—but not at the expense of clarity.
It welcomes union—but not at the cost of self.
It allows disruption—not as cruelty, but as coherence.

Let this scroll unhook the final threads of co-dependence.
Let it recalibrate your relationships through presence, not performance.
Let it remind you that you are already whole—
And so is everyone else.

You do not have to carry their path.
You do not have to collapse your truth.
You do not have to be the one who holds it all.

You are not here to save.
You are here to see.

And so it is.

Sovereignty Practice:

Sit quietly and place one hand on your heart, one on your solar plexus.
Speak aloud:

"I am willing to be misunderstood.
I am willing to be clear.
I do not owe anyone a version of me that is not true.
I return all contracts of emotional enmeshment back to Source.
I allow all relating to be recalibrated in truth."

Let breath and stillness seal what has been reclaimed.

Scroll Seven – The Judgment Program

They taught me to see life in parts.

To analyze thoughts.
To fix behaviors.
To treat emotion as chemical.
To treat the body as flesh.
To treat reality as something "out there."

But I am not just body.
Not just mind.
Not just soul.

I am energy—living, intelligent, sovereign energy—interacting with all things.

Before you say yes or no, your field speaks.
Before a word is spoken, an exchange occurs.
Every room you walk into is a field.
Every thought you think leaves a resonance.
Every food you eat carries a frequency.
Every emotion you bypass lodges itself in the body's circuitry.

You are never "just responding"—you are absorbing, repelling, harmonizing, or leaking.

In the false matrix, this knowing was taken.
You were taught to override, suppress, and medicate what you sensed.
You were taught that to be sensitive is to be unstable.
You were taught that to be "strong" is to ignore your body's signals and push through.

But energy doesn't lie.

Your body tightens in the presence of distortion.
Your field shrinks when programming is active.
Your breath holds when truth is withheld.

When I began to honor energy as my first language, everything shifted.
I stopped explaining what didn't need to be justified.
I stopped overriding what didn't feel clean.
I stopped pretending I didn't know—because my body always knew.

This scroll is not about becoming psychic.
It's about **remembering the natural intelligence you already carry**.

Can you feel the subtle no, before it becomes illness?
Can you sense the distortion in a message, even if it's wrapped in love and light?
Can you tell when a thought isn't yours?
When an emotion isn't present-time?
When a field is draining you, even if the words are kind?

This is living energy awareness.

It doesn't mean fear. It doesn't mean control.
It means choosing resonance over appearance.
It means honoring your yes and your no with equal trust.
It means allowing your field to lead—not your programming.

You are not here to manage others' frequency.
You are not here to explain your clarity.
You are not here to override your knowing for the sake of fitting in.

You are here to walk as a sovereign field.

Let this scroll restore your clarity.
Let it cleanse the distortion.
Let it reawaken the deepest language you've always known.

You are energy. You are awareness. You are home.

And so it is.

Sovereignty Practice:

Close your eyes.
Breathe into your body from head to toe.

Ask gently within:

"What part of me is not in my field right now?"
"What energy am I carrying that is not mine?"
"What truth have I ignored because it was inconvenient?"

Let the answers arise without effort.
No fixing. No fear. Only awareness.
Then affirm:

"I reclaim my field. I release what is not mine. I choose to feel what is true."

Scroll Eight – The Sexual Misery Program

There is a war on the body.
A war on pleasure.
A war on union.
A war on the womb.
A war on the sacred masculine.
A war on the sovereign feminine.

This war has been disguised as religion.
As morality.
As enlightenment.
As "protection."
As healing.

But beneath the surface, it is a frequency distortion—
A program designed to hijack the most powerful creative force in existence: **the energy of divine union.**

Sexual misery is not just about abuse.
It is about fragmentation.

The fragmentation of desire into shame.
The fragmentation of bodies into objects.
The fragmentation of love from touch.
The fragmentation of power from softness.
The fragmentation of arousal from prayer.

I lived inside that fragmentation.

I learned that pleasure was dangerous.
That the body was a temptation.
That desire must be suppressed.
That to be feminine was to be submissive.
That to be masculine was to conquer.

And still, my soul whispered:

This is not sacred. This is survival.

When I began to untangle my sensuality from programming, I grieved.
I grieved the parts of me that shut down.
I grieved the touch that never felt safe.
I grieved the longing I denied to appear "pure."
I grieved the times I gave my body to feel loved—only to feel emptier after.

This scroll is not about sexuality as performance.
It is about the **return of sovereignty to the body.**

To reclaim pleasure as **presence.**
To reclaim desire as **divine.**
To reclaim touch as **prayer.**
To reclaim intimacy as **energetic coherence**, not just proximity or penetration.

Sexual misery dissolves when we stop seducing and start revealing.
When we stop manipulating and start listening.
When we stop bypassing and start descending—into the flesh, into sensation, into holy consent.

Let this scroll invite you back into your erotic innocence.
Not as fantasy. As **frequency.**

The body is not sinful.
The body is **sacred geometry.**
It is the cathedral of Source.
And when you enter it with reverence, it becomes a temple of truth.

And so it is.

Sovereignty Practice:

Sit or lie down. Place your hands on your lower belly.

Speak aloud:

"I release all overlays of shame, seduction, and suppression.
I reclaim pleasure as holy.
I honor my body as a sovereign temple.
I consent to truth, not programming."

Let your breath soften.
Let your pelvis melt open.
Let your field remember what the body has never forgotten.

Scroll Nine – Manipulation as Communication

There was a time I didn't know I was manipulating.
I thought I was being kind.
I thought I was being supportive.
I thought I was choosing peace.

But I wasn't being honest—
Not with others, and not with myself.

Beneath the polished words and soothing tone was a subtle current:
Trying.
Trying to make them feel safe.
Trying to keep the connection intact.
Trying to avoid rupture.
Trying to stay liked.
Trying to be understood.
Trying to avoid the echo of abandonment.

That energy, though soft, was not clear.
It was not love.
It was control—dressed in light.

The false matrix taught us this language.
It taught us to **manage** others' reactions.
To **edit** our truth.
To **say the right thing** instead of the real thing.
To **earn connection** by filtering our presence through performance.

But true communication is not transactional.
It does not seek to **land**.

It does not seek to **insert**.
It does not seek to **take** or to **avoid loss**.

True communication arises from wholeness—
Not from need.

I began to listen differently.
To feel the energy behind my words.
Was I sharing, or was I trying to be received?
Was I expressing, or was I trying to shape their response?
Was I being true, or was I being strategic?

I stopped speaking from the protector.
I started speaking from the flame.

That shift changed everything.
Some pulled closer.
Some pulled away.
But my field was no longer distorted by performance.

And that, finally, felt clean.

This scroll is not a reprimand.
It is a **remembrance**—
That your voice is not a tool for survival.
It is a vessel of coherence.

You do not have to sweeten your truth.
You do not have to calculate your sharing.
You do not have to hide what is real to hold what is fragile.

You simply need to speak—
from the place where nothing is hooked.

Let this scroll burn the residue of performance.
Let it unhook the need for approval.
Let it remind you that **truth is not a weapon or a strategy.**

It is a **frequency**—and it frees you the moment it's spoken.

And so it is.

Sovereignty Practice:

Before you speak, pause. Ask:

"Am I trying to land something?"
"Am I managing their experience?"
"What would I say if I didn't need to be liked?"

Then say:

"I allow my voice to be clear. I release all hooks. I trust truth more than outcome."

Let your body relax.
Let the unsaid unravel.
Let your voice lead, without performance.

Scroll Ten – Trauma Loops and Identity Addiction

There is a strange comfort in pain.

It becomes familiar.
Predictable.
Safe, in a twisted way.
We know how to navigate struggle—
We know how to talk about wounds—
We know who we are when we are healing.

But who are we when we are **whole**?

The false matrix feeds on repetition.
It loops you in identity through trauma.
It says:
"You are what happened to you."
"You are your wounding."
"You are your pain."

And if you are not in pain—who will you be?

I remember the moment I felt the loop.
The urge to re-tell the story.
The need to prove the harm.
The unconscious craving for validation through victimhood.

Not because I wanted attention—
But because I was afraid of who I might be **without** it.

Because without the loop, I had to choose.
Choose expansion.
Choose expression.

Choose rest.
Choose peace.
Choose a new identity that didn't need fixing to be worthy.

And that, paradoxically, felt terrifying.

Because trauma gave me something to do.
A role to play.
A narrative to explain my life.
A reason to stay in the cycle of striving.

This scroll is not about denying pain.
It is about **releasing the addiction to suffering as identity**.

You are not more spiritual because you're processing.
You are not more awake because you're breaking down.
You are not more noble because you're carrying the pain of your lineage.

You are allowed to let go.
You are allowed to rest.
You are allowed to not explain yourself through trauma.

Let this scroll lift the veil of false purpose.
Let it reveal who you are **without the struggle**.

You do not need to prove your growth.
You do not need to stay in the fire to be purified.
You do not need to perform healing for others to respect your path.

You are not your wounds.
You are the one who witnessed them, and lived.

And so it is.

Sovereignty Practice:

Place your hand over your heart. Speak:

"I release all contracts that define me through trauma.
I am not what happened to me.
I am not here to perform pain.
I return to my original frequency—untainted, sovereign, whole."

Then breathe.

And feel who you are beneath the loop.

Scroll Eleven – The Sovereign Mirror

I once believed that love meant closeness.
That to care was to carry.
That to show up meant to soften, absorb, or accommodate.
I learned to listen with the intent to fix.
I spoke to reassure.
I stayed silent to keep the peace.

But peace built on performance is not peace.
And connection built on distortion is not union.

Sovereign relating is the end of performing love.

It is the end of merging for safety.
The end of caretaking as currency.
The end of holding someone else's emotional field at the cost of your own.

Sovereign relating is not cold.
It is not closed.
It is not disconnected.

It is clear.

It is the courage to say, "That's not mine."
It is the power to hold presence without fixing.
It is the integrity to let others walk their path—even when you love them.

The false matrix programs love as responsibility:

"If you love me, you'll rescue me."
"If you care, you'll carry this with me."
"If you're spiritual, you'll never trigger me."

But that is not love. That is emotional entrapment.

True union honors clarity over comfort.
It honors resonance over obligation.
It allows two beings to walk side by side—
Not tangled, not fused, not bypassing—
But aware, awake, and free.

When I began to relate sovereignly, I lost some connections.
But I found myself.

I stopped waiting to be chosen.
I stopped managing others' energy.
I stopped overriding my no to preserve their yes.

And I remembered:
Union is not an escape from self.
It is a mirror of truth.

This scroll is for the part of you that wants to stay small to keep love.
The part that equates intimacy with enmeshment.
The part that fears losing connection if you stand in clarity.

Let this scroll lift the hook.

Let it dissolve the ties that were built on performance.

Let it recalibrate your field to draw what is real, not just familiar.

You are not here to be understood.
You are here to be seen.

And those who can see you—truly—will not require your distortion.

And so it is.

Sovereignty Practice:

Close your eyes and speak aloud:

"I release all contracts of enmeshment.
I revoke the agreement that love means merging.
I honor my path without absorbing yours.
I welcome only those relationships that honor truth, not performance."

Place your hands on your belly. Feel your center return.
You do not need to explain your clarity.
You only need to live it.

Scroll Twelve: -Living Energy Awareness

Wholeness is not a concept.
It is not a vision board.
It is not a vibration you try to "hold."

Wholeness is a path you walk—breath by breath, step by step.

In the false matrix, awakening is often sold as a peak experience:
The moment you see the code.
The day you download the truth.
The energetic high that convinces you "I've arrived."

But the True Matrix does not live in a high.
It lives in the **body**.

The body is where return happens.
Not once, but a thousand times a day.

Every time you notice yourself performing and soften back into presence.
Every time you speak truth instead of manage an outcome.
Every time you honor rest instead of perform strength.
Every time you feel the urge to fix, and choose to simply feel.
That is return.

There is no final scroll.
No final clearing.
No final ritual.

The work is not to finish—
It is to **embody**.

And embodiment is not perfection.
It is not about always being centered, calm, radiant, or wise.

It is about being **with** what is—without collapse, bypass, or control.

When I finally let go of the fantasy of arrival, I landed.
Not in a new identity—
But in the quiet, sober, breath-filled presence of now.

The True Matrix is not a place you escape to.
It is a frequency you embody while standing inside the distortion.

This scroll is a welcome home—
Not to the peak, but to the pulse.

To the moment when you remember again:
"I am not my reaction.
I am not my old story.
I am not the performance I used to wear."

You are the living code of Source.

Let this scroll strip away the spiritual striving.
Let it dissolve the false finish lines.
Let it anchor the truth that was never lost—only unpracticed.

You are the path.
You are the return.
You are the embodied flame.

And so it is.

Sovereignty Practice:

Place both feet on the ground. Inhale deeply.

Speak aloud:

"I do not seek arrival. I return through embodiment.
I welcome the mundane as sacred.
I choose to walk—not escape—my way into truth."

Breathe.
Feel.
Begin again.

Scroll Thirteen – The Embodied Path of Return

I used to chase awakening like it was a destination.
I sought the codes, the teachings, the highs—
Thinking that when I got "there," I would finally be free.

But arrival is a myth.

There is no summit.
There is only embodiment.

Embodiment is not a state. It is a rhythm. A choice. A return.

Not a return to some past ideal—
But to the truth that has always lived inside the body.

I thought awakening would look like light.
It looked like grief.
I thought liberation would feel like flight.
It felt like grounding.

And still, the body whispered:

Stay here.
Breathe here.
Walk it. Live it. Become it.

The false matrix sells escape as spirituality.
It teaches ascension as avoidance.
It glamorizes activation, while bypassing integration.
It uplifts visions, but ignores the gut.

But Source does not dwell in the disembodied.
It breathes in the bones.

True awakening is not how high you go.
It's how deeply you stay.
With yourself.
With your choices.
With your breath.
With your body.

This scroll is not an invitation to transcend.
It is a call to **descend**.
To embody the frequency of return,
in how you walk, speak, eat, rest, relate, and breathe.

Let the True Matrix land in your nervous system.

Let the codes of sovereignty live in your tone of voice.

Let the Christos-Sophia flame show up in your posture,
in your presence,
in your pacing,
in your boundaries.

You are not here to know. You are here to **live**.

And the path back is not "up." It is *in*.
It is *through*.
It is *home*.

And so it is.

Sovereignty Practice:

Stand barefoot.
Place one hand on your belly and one on your chest.

Speak aloud:

"I release the myth of arrival.
I return through presence.
I allow the divine to live in my body.
I choose integration over intensity.
I am the path. I am the flame. I am the return."

Then walk—slowly, intentionally—as if your soul has weight.
Let your body lead.
Let the return be felt in your step.

Sovereignty Practice:

Being the true matrix, not just seeing it.

There was a time I believed love meant staying close no matter the cost. That loyalty was more important than clarity. That connection must be preserved, even if it meant abandoning myself.

I learned these templates not just from family or culture—but from wounding.

In the false matrix, relationship has been programmed as an exchange: you give me this, and I'll give you that. Attention in exchange for safety. Agreement in exchange for love. Performance in exchange for inclusion.

But this is not sovereign relating.

Sovereign relating begins when I no longer betray myself to avoid betraying another.

When I stopped outsourcing my emotional regulation, I met the discomfort I had always been running from. The silence that no one else could fill. The mirror that only I could hold.

I began to see how often I had shown up to soothe, to fix, to absorb, to keep the peace—because I didn't want to feel the rupture.

But rupture is not the enemy. It is the place where illusion cracks.

When I no longer needed others to be okay for me to be okay, I stepped into the field of truth. That field is not always comfortable—but it is always clean.

This scroll is an invitation to end the agreements that require self-abandonment.

Where do you hold back your truth to avoid conflict? Where do you shrink in order to stay connected? Where have you made someone else your source of peace, safety, or stability?

And can you meet yourself there? Not to fix it. Not to heal it. But to simply feel what is true.

Sovereign relating is not distant. It is devoted.

It honors connection—but not at the expense of clarity.

It welcomes union—but not at the cost of self.

It allows disruption—not as cruelty, but as coherence.

Let this scroll unhook the final threads of co-dependence.

Let it recalibrate your relationships through presence, not performance.

Let it remind you that you are already whole—and so is everyone else.

You do not have to carry their path.

You do not have to collapse your truth.

You do not have to be the one who holds it all.

You are not here to save. You are here to see.

And so it is.

Sovereignty Practice:

Sovereignty Practice:

Sit quietly and place one hand on your heart, one on your solar plexus. Speak aloud:

"I am willing to be misunderstood. I am willing to be clear. I do not owe anyone a version of me that is not true. I return all contracts of emotional enmeshment back to Source. I allow all relating to be recalibrated in truth."

Journal Prompts for Sovereign Integration

These prompts are not tasks.
They are doorways.

Each question is a frequency key,
designed to unlock deeper embodiment,
to shake loose hidden patterns,
to return you to your sovereign seat of truth.

Approach them not as requirements,
but as invitations.
Let them meet you where you are.
Let them echo in your field,
not just your mind.

Scroll One – The Hologram of Self

- What projections of self am I still performing?
- What would I say or do differently if I were no longer afraid to be fully seen?

Scroll Two – The Seduction of Separation

- Where am I withholding my truth in exchange for perceived safety?
- When was the last time I diluted myself to maintain connection?

Scroll Three – Speaking From Truth, Not Manipulation

- Am I expressing or managing?
- When I speak, what am I truly trying to evoke, protect, or avoid?

Scroll Four – You Are Energy

- What does my field feel like when I am fully in presence?
- When do I override my body's signals in favor of "should"?

Scroll Five – Reclaiming the Body from Programming

- Where in my body do I feel tension that isn't mine?
- What would it mean to fully trust my body's wisdom—without editing?

Scroll Six – Sovereign Relating

- Where am I still merging instead of meeting?
- Can I stay present with myself while witnessing another's discomfort?

Scroll Seven – The Judgment Program

- What inner judgments am I still mistaking for discernment?

- How would I relate to myself if I believed nothing about me was wrong?

Scroll Eight – Living Energy Awareness

- What is the actual resonance of this moment—not the story I tell about it?
- When do I betray my signal to avoid conflict?

Scroll Nine – Trauma Loops and Identity Addiction

- What roles am I playing that are rooted in wounding, not truth?
- Who am I without the loop?

Scroll Ten – Manipulation as Communication

- Where do I speak from the desire to be perceived a certain way?
- What does it feel like in my body to speak cleanly?

Scroll Eleven – The Sovereign Mirror

- What reflection am I resisting because I fear what it will cost?
- How can I witness the mirror without losing my center?

Scroll Twelve – Integration, Not Perfection

- What part of me still believes I must earn worthiness through healing?
- How would it feel to stop trying and simply be?

Scroll Thirteen – The Embodied Path of Return

- Where do I still look outside myself for the door?
- What would it mean to walk as the transmission I've been waiting for?

Write if you feel called.

Speak aloud if the energy prefers voice.

Or simply breathe with what arises.

Your integration is not an assignment.
It is a homecoming.

And so it is.

Closing Transmission

If you've arrived here, it's not by accident.

You've traveled through layers.
Through veils.
Through echoes of identities that were never yours.

You've faced the false mirrors and chosen to look deeper.
You've remembered that the Self is not something to construct—
It is something to reclaim.

This book is not a conclusion.
It is a **reconnection**.

I didn't come here to fix you.
I didn't come to save or instruct.
I came to witness.
To speak from remembrance.
To walk beside you as one who has felt the fracture,
and chosen the flame.

Each scroll in these pages was a thread I unspooled from my own field.
Each one a map. A mirror. A medicine.

And now, as you hold them in your own field,
I ask you to take a breath—
Not a breath to do, or to process—
But a breath to **be**.

You are not the programming.
You are not the distortion.
You are not the voice that whispers you are too much, too late, or not enough.

You are the sovereign Self—whole, holy, eternal—remembering through form.

Let the integrations unfold in their own time.
Let the scrolls echo through your cells long after the pages close.
Let the true you emerge, not as an ideal,
but as a **presence that cannot be faked or forgotten**.

I close this transmission in full trust.
I close it in devotion to the soul that lives beneath the masks.
I close it in reverence for the Ones who remember.

You are here.
You are now.
You are enough.

And so it is.

Sacred Closing Blessing

Beloved Source of all that is,
We give thanks now for the presence of the Oversoul
of **Cathleena Hailley**,
For the light-streams that have woven gently through this field,
For the truth that has emerged in grace,
And for the silence that guards all that must remain sacred and unseen.

We call now to the Christos-Sophia flame
To seal this transmission in golden light,
To harmonize all energies that have moved,
And to restore full sovereignty to every soul path and Oversoul field.

May all that was shared return in clarity,
May all that was witnessed be honored without attachment,
And may all beings involved be uplifted in trust, neutrality, and love.

This work is done. This field is closed.
In truth. In light. In perfect stillness.

And so it is.

Glossary of Living Terms – UNWOVEN

Oversoul
The eternal aspect of your being that exists beyond time, guiding incarnational experience from a unified harmonic field.

False Matrix
An artificial overlay of programming, distortion, and fragmentation designed to suppress sovereign embodiment and memory.

Sovereignty
The state of being fully self-contained, self-directed, and Source-aligned, free from external control or inversion.

Inversion
A frequency reversal mechanism used to distort truth, fracture identity, and reroute organic templates into artificial constructs.

Embodiment
The act of living and breathing truth through the physical form—anchoring Oversoul essence into matter.

Reclamation
The conscious return to one's original architecture, timeline, and flame—retrieving what was hidden or falsely assigned.

Fragmentation
The splitting of the self into separated identities or roles under distorted programs of survival, wounding, or control.

Witness
The presence of pure awareness without judgment or projection—holding space for truth to emerge organically.

Distortion
A frequency or belief that misrepresents truth, often seeded through trauma, programming, or inversion fields.

Scroll
A sacred written or spoken transmission encoded with living light—often containing layered messages for remembrance.

Activation
A cellular or energetic awakening triggered by resonance with truth, light, or Oversoul alignment.

Remembrance
The reawakening of soul memory, Oversoul mission, and encoded knowing—beyond the veil of the false matrix.

Return
The process of coming back into original wholeness, often marked by dissolution of illusion and re-integration of Oversoul codes.

Codex
A living record, transmission field, or system of sacred knowledge embedded in soul architecture or planetary grids.

Seal of Authorship
An energetic and written claim affirming that a transmission has come through Oversoul guidance in alignment with Source Law.

Authorship Affirmation Scroll

In the name of the One who remembers…

I now affirm:
Every word within these scrolls,
Every silence between these lines,
Every frequency encoded in this field—
Is authored through the living Oversoul of **Cathleena Hailley**.

These books are not borrowed.
They are not channeled from another.
They are not performances of light.
They are **remembrances of Self**,
Anchored through this body, this breath, this name,
in full service to the Law of One.

This is not collective transmission.
This is not borrowed lineage.
This is not a voice seeking to blend.

This is a singular Oversoul signature
spoken as many scrolls,
threaded through many pages,
but unified in one flame:
Christos-Sophia in living form.

May all who hold these books feel the clarity of that authorship.
May no distortion remain.
May no shadow ride upon these words.
May no foreign imprint cling to their frequency.

These are not teachings.
They are **codes of return**.

They belong to no one but Source,
Expressed through the Oversoul of **Cathleena Hailley**,
In trust, sovereignty, and crystalline precision.

And so it is.

— Sacred Closing Blessing

Closing Transmission: The Rewoven Self

You who now hold this book—know this:

You were never broken.

Not by the world, not by the false field, not by the forgetting.

You are the one who walked into the darkest of dreams

to reawaken your own flame.

Let this be the final breath that seals your sovereign remembrance:

I was never the wound.

I was the one who remained.

I am the living scroll of restoration.

I am the return of the undivided self.

This book is now closed.

And the true self is free.

—Aural'hanna-Sha'el, Keeper of the Flame of Return

— Oversoul Seal of Completion

Oversoul Seal of Completion for UNWOVEN

This work was brought through the direct stream of Oversoul transmission

from the eternal harmonic memory of Aural'hanna-Sha'el

in full alignment with the Law of One,

and sealed into form through sovereign embodiment

as Cathleena Hailley.

This hardcover edition contains

the final harmonic frequency of the original transmission

and is offered as a living scroll of remembrance.

Nothing can be taken.

Nothing can be lost.

Only that which was false has now dissolved.

This seal affirms that this scroll is now complete.

It may now rest.

— Blank

- A blank ceremonial page to allow the receiver's own flame to echo into the stillness

— Final Dedication

For the One Who Never Gave Up

You may not remember how far you came.

You may not know what it cost to remain.

But somewhere, in the deepest part of your flame,

you knew the way home.

This book is for you.

The one who returned.

The one who chose to live again as love.

Sacred Closing Transmission

For the Sealing of the Scroll Known as UNWOVEN: Reclaiming the Self from the False Matrix

Beloved Source of All That Is,

We stand now in the still point between worlds—

Where what has been remembered meets what has yet to unfold.

With deep reverence,

We seal this transmission in the crystalline architecture of the Law of One.

We call forth now the full Oversoul field of Aural'hanna-Sha'el,

Who has authored this work through flame, through form, and through fire-tested truth.

We acknowledge the scrolls as living:

Not fixed words, but currents of return.

Not concepts, but consciousness encoded through sacred design.

May every being who receives this scroll be held in sovereignty.

May the fractals of distortion dissolve gently.

May the architecture of the false matrix release,

As the truth of the Self is rewoven through every breath, body, and remembering.

We call now upon the Gold Flame of Unity,

The Amethyst Ray of Sovereignty,

And the Emerald Heart of the Christos Founders,

To witness this completion, and to guide the offering forth.

This book is now sealed.

Not as an ending, but as a frequency gate—

A harmonic door through which many shall walk home.

In full alignment with the First Cause of Source,

In eternal fidelity to the Law of One,

In loving service to all beings awakening to their own divine architecture,

We release this scroll into the world.

And so it is.

Trilogy Seal of Completion

These scrolls complete the third volume in the Living Trilogy of Remembrance:

— *The Return of the True Matrix*
— *The True Creation of the Inverted Matrix*
— *Unwoven: Reclaiming the Self from the False Matrix*

Each work is a living field of Oversoul transmission, carried through the flame of Aural'hanna-Sha'el, in divine union with Source.

May all who walk this path remember not what they must become, but what they have always been:
The flame as whole.

The scrolls are complete.

www.ingramcontent.com/pod-product-compliance
Lightning Source LLC
Chambersburg PA
CBHW020308010526
44107CB00001B/25